# ENDANGE...

# Animals
## of the Jungle

William B. Rice

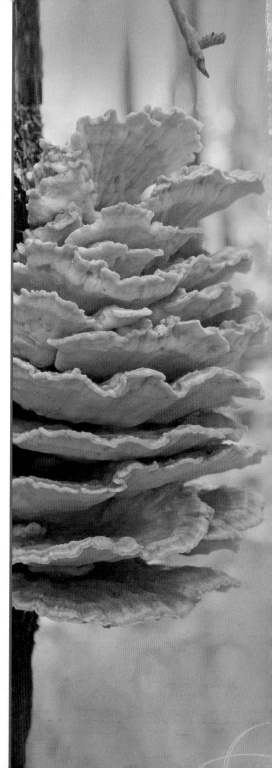

## Consultants

**Timothy Rasinski, Ph.D.**
Kent State University

**Lori Oczkus**
Literacy Consultant

**Thorsten Pape**
Animal Trainer

**Based on** writing from
*TIME For Kids. TIME For Kids* and the *TIME For Kids* logo are registered trademarks of TIME Inc. Used under license.

### Publishing Credits

Dona Herweck Rice, *Editor-in-Chief*
Lee Aucoin, *Creative Director*
Jamey Acosta, *Senior Editor*
Heidi Fiedler, *Editor*
Lexa Hoang, *Designer*
Stephanie Reid, *Photo Editor*
Rachelle Cracchiolo, *M.S.Ed., Publisher*

### Teacher Created Materials

5301 Oceanus Drive
Huntington Beach, CA 92649-1030
http://www.tcmpub.com
**ISBN 978-1-4333-4937-9**

# TABLE OF CONTENTS

# LIFELESS

The jungle is alive. Alive with plants. Alive with animals. Alive with sound, color, motion, and fragrance. It pulses and breathes as though the jungle itself were a single living thing.

More **species** than can be imagined live in the thick foliage of the world's jungles. But year by year—even day by day—more and more species simply cease to exist. Left unprotected, what was once filled with life becomes silent, gray, and still.

Lifeless. **Extinct.**

red-eyed tree frog

black-and-white lemur ≫

# THINK LINK

- What animals live in the world's jungles?
- In what ways are they in danger?
- How can we protect them?

toucan

# ENDANGERED

Over time, Earth changes. In some areas, it gets warmer and wetter. In others, it may get drier or colder. It is natural that some species are unable to handle these changes. They cannot **thrive** and prosper. At some point, they cease to be. But more and more, the effects of human actions weaken otherwise healthy species. They become **endangered**, or in danger of dying off. Sometimes, they become extinct, or wiped from the planet.

Some people think it's merely sad when a species becomes endangered and extinct. They're sorry that humans will no longer see that species. But the truth is, "sad" is the least of the problem. All species depend on one another. The loss of a single species can have tragic results for all.

kapok flower

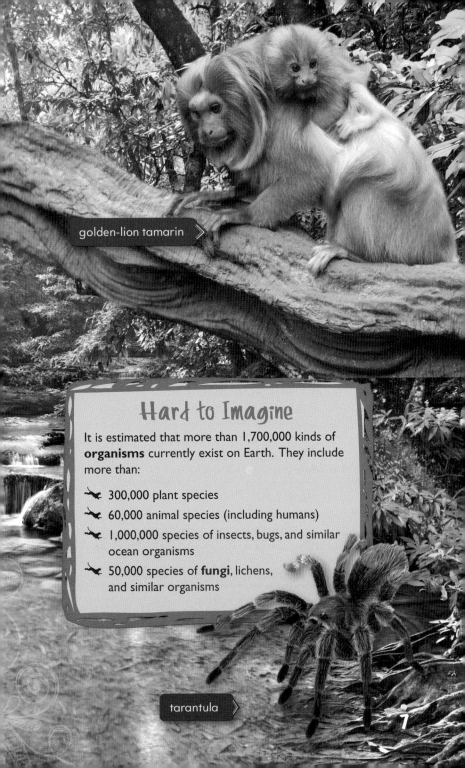

golden-lion tamarin

## Hard to Imagine

It is estimated that more than 1,700,000 kinds of **organisms** currently exist on Earth. They include more than:

- 300,000 plant species
- 60,000 animal species (including humans)
- 1,000,000 species of insects, bugs, and similar ocean organisms
- 50,000 species of **fungi**, lichens, and similar organisms

tarantula

# SPECIES

A species is a type of life form. Panthers, toucans, and kapok trees are all types of species. Throughout history, there have been millions of species on Earth. Life has existed for many hundreds of millions of years. Different species prosper at different times in different ways. And sometimes, they naturally fade away.

| | | |
|---|---|---|
| **Kingdom** | The largest group of living things can be classified into kingdom *Animalia*. | |
| **Phylum** | Only some of these animals can be classified as *Chordata*. They have backbones. | |
| **Class** | Mammals belong to the class *Mammalia*. Most mammals have hair and nourish their young with milk. | |
| **Order** | **Taxonomy** divides each group into smaller groups. Those animals in order *Carnivora* eat only meat. | |
| **Family** | Every living thing goes into a category at each level. The family *Felidae* is made up of different types of cats. | |
| **Genus** | The genus name is the first word in the scientific name of a creature. | |
| **Species** | This chart shows that a tiger falls in *Animalia*, *Chordata*, *Mammalia*, *Carnivora*, *Felidae*, *Panthera*, and *Panthera Tigris*. | |

The planet is rich with many forms of life. Plants, animals, insects, and fungi all coexist. They live within a system in which all species depend on one another. Humans, too, depend on other forms of life. No species stands on its own. And what happens to one species affects many others.

## Species Breakdown

Taxonomy is a way to organize living things into groups based on how they are related. All species fall into one of six broad kingdoms. The species name is the most specific way to describe a plant or animal. A species is a group of living things made up of individuals that can produce **fertile** offspring. Scientists usually identify animals by their genus and species name, as in *Panthera tigris*.

# Interdependence

It would take pages and pages in a book to show how all species on Earth are connected to one another. It may even be impossible. But here's a small sample that shows how some species depend on one another simply for food. This is a small sample of a jungle food web, showing how the different species depend on one another for survival. Due to **deforestation**, this whole system is in danger of collapse.

Larger animals, such as cheetahs, eat smaller animals, such as baboons.

Plants serve as food for many animals such as insects, antelope, and birds.

STOP! THINK...

- Which creatures provide energy to others?
- Which plants or animals are most dependent on other creatures?
- What might happen if one of the lower creatures is removed from the web?

Animals with a varied diet are better able to survive changes in their environment. Animals that feed on just one type of plant or animal can easily beome endangered.

# DANGEROUS FACTORS

There are many different causes for endangerment. But they can be grouped into just a few main factors. Sometimes, a natural **habitat** is changed to the point at which it cannot support the **native** species. This often comes from human activity. Such activities may include cutting down trees for wood products, growing crops, or making way for roads and houses.

Overexploitation is the overuse of a **renewable** resource so it cannot be **sustained**, or kept going. Overgrazing, overfishing, and overlogging are all types of overexploitation.

## It's Alive!

The peccary looks like a pig, but it's not. The peccary was thought to be extinct in 1930, when **fossils** of the species were found but none were seen living. Then, in 1975, one was found alive in Paraguay. There are thought to be about 3,000 of these hairy beasties alive today.

## Extirpation

When a species is wiped out from an area in which it used to exist but it still exists elsewhere, it is extinct locally, or **extirpated**. Often, extirpation is a sign of endangerment, but not always. A local catastrophe might cause extirpation. For example, some species have been extirpated after major volcanic eruptions.

# Going Native

It's troubling when species disappear, but adding species can damage land as well. Non-native species may be introduced to an area when people bring in plants and animals from other areas of the world. It can be an accident or intentional. The new species can take over areas and change the balance of life that is natural to the area. Also, non-native species may spread much farther and faster than they would in their native area because their natural predators are not present to balance the **population**. The animals below are examples of destructive non-native species.

## Nutria Rat

The nutria rat, a semiaquatic rodent, was brought to Louisiana in the 1930s. Originally from South America, this non-native species has created *big* problems for coastal wetlands. Nutria rats have a fierce appetite for the marsh roots that make up coastal wetlands and provide important barriers against storms. Even worse, the rodents reproduce very quickly. There are more than 20 million in the United States.

## Asian Carp

Asian carp were brought to the United States from Asia to clean algae from fish farms. But because of flooding, the Asian carp were let loose and spread quickly. Their diet endangers native fish like the bass and the crappie that consume the same food.

## European Rabbit

European rabbits are a big threat in Australia. They have affected native species as well as Australian **agriculture**. Brought to Australia in the 1700s, the rabbits have destroyed the land, causing millions of dollars in lost crops. By eating all of the plants in the area, they have also caused **erosion** and prevented native species from feeding.

# AFRICAN JUNGLES

When people think of tropical temperatures, dense plant life, and **exotic** creatures, they often think of African jungles. But in the jungles of Africa, as in jungles everywhere, some of the world's most extraordinary animal species are in serious danger.

# EASTERN MOUNTAIN GORILLA

The mountain gorilla is endangered. Experts estimate there are only 790 left. The gorilla is truly a majestic animal. The male can grow to just over six feet tall. Its arms span over seven feet wide. It can weigh nearly 500 pounds! The gorilla moves by walking on its knuckles. It mainly stays on the ground but will climb into trees for fruit if the tree will support its weight. Gorillas rest for long periods in the middle of the day.

## Home and Family

Gorillas live in cold, misty mountain forests. They live in small groups of up to 30 individuals. The males defend the group. Babies sleep with their mothers in nests. If a mother within a group dies or leaves, the oldest male will look after her **abandoned** offspring, even allowing the baby to sleep in his nest.

# Silverbacks

Males are called *silverbacks* because the hair on their backs turns silver or gray with age. Silverbacks are very strong and powerful. When two silverbacks encounter each other, they may fight. Their powerful jaws can cut deep gaping wounds. But these great beasts can be gentle with the young of their group. Young gorillas wrestle and chase each other, turn somersaults, and even engage the silverback, who gently tolerates and even encourages the play.

What are the biggest threats to these intelligent creatures? They are **poached** for their heads, hands, and feet as trophies. Babies are captured and sold as pets. Their habitats are being lost to human settlement. They suffer from diseases spread by humans and farm animals. Even human wars have led to gorilla deaths.

Silverbacks caught in traps are sometimes able to remove the traps from their hands or feet.

## Big Eaters!

Gorillas mainly eat plants. Males can eat up to 75 pounds of vegetation a day, while females can eat up to 40 pounds a day.

The endangered eastern lowland gorilla is similar to the mountain gorilla. Only about 5,000 remain in the wild. Twenty-four of these beautiful animals were counted in zoos.

# AFRICAN LEOPARD

The African leopard is rare outside its protected areas. And its numbers are declining. Leopards live alone, although females live with their cubs. Leopards are most active at night when they do most of their hunting. They have been found to live in many different types of habitats, from rainforests to deserts to grasslands. They have even been seen high up in the mountains.

## Beautiful Coats

Leopards are not exactly spotted, but rather their coats have black rosettes. Rosettes are groupings of dark spots around a lighter central area. The main part of the coat will vary from pale yellow to deep gold or tawny depending on the leopard's habitat. The coloring on the coat serves as **camouflage**. Some leopards may be completely black. These leopards are often called *black panthers*.

## Caching

Leopards are excellent climbers. They often place the animals they kill—even very large ones such as giraffes or antelope—up in trees. Caching makes it very difficult for other animals to take the dead animal away from the leopard.

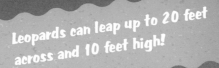
Leopards can leap up to 20 feet across and 10 feet high!

Leopards are very good, **agile**, and patient hunters with strong jaws and long claws. They are cunning and stealthy, and prefer to get close to their prey before pouncing.

How can these agile hunters with such an instinct for survival be at risk? The danger they face is from humans. They suffer habitat loss through human settlement. They are killed because humans see them as a threat to their farm animals. And often, they are hunted as trophies.

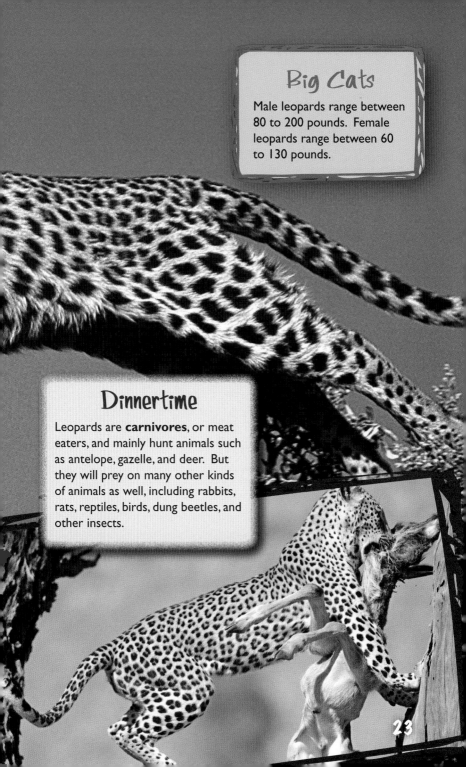

## Big Cats

Male leopards range between 80 to 200 pounds. Female leopards range between 60 to 130 pounds.

## Dinnertime

Leopards are **carnivores**, or meat eaters, and mainly hunt animals such as antelope, gazelle, and deer. But they will prey on many other kinds of animals as well, including rabbits, rats, reptiles, birds, dung beetles, and other insects.

# MANDRILL

The mandrill is the largest monkey species and is similar to a baboon. It mainly lives in rainforests. Female mandrills live in large groups called *hordes*. The hordes usually have hundreds of members. Males live a more solitary life. They only join a horde during mating season. The mandrill is at risk because it is being hunted for its meat. Its homes are also being destroyed by humans.

While mandrills spend most of their time on the ground, at night they sleep in trees.

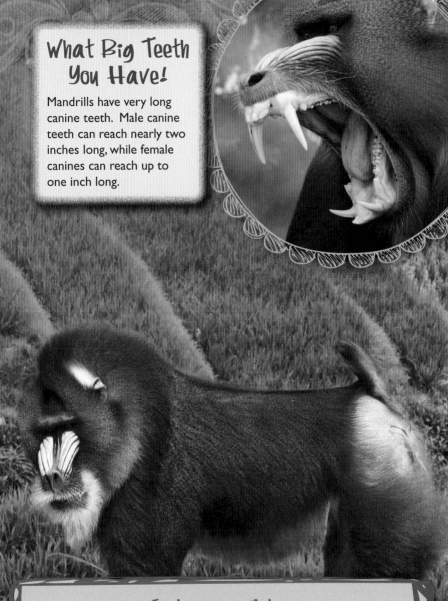

## What Big Teeth You Have!

Mandrills have very long canine teeth. Male canine teeth can reach nearly two inches long, while female canines can reach up to one inch long.

## In Living Color

The mandrill is probably the most colorful **primate** in the world. It has a dark green or grey coat with yellow and black bands and a white belly. Its hairless face has a red stripe down the middle, with blue ridges on the sides. It has red nostrils and lips, a yellow beard, and white tufts of hair near the ears. Its bottom is red, pink, blue, and purple.

# CHIMPANZEE

Chimpanzees, or chimps, live in large groups. They communicate with sounds, gestures, and facial expressions. Chimps use tools such as rocks, sticks, grass, and leaves. They use them mainly to get water and food. They also sharpen and modify sticks to make better tools. Chimps live in many habitats. But they mainly live where there are lots of trees. They make nests for sleeping. Chimps like to eat fruit and other plant parts. They eat insects, birds, eggs, and small animals—even monkeys. The biggest threats to chimps are habitat destruction, poaching, and disease. The building of new roads has damaged habitats and

## Big Guy

The adult chimpanzee can be about the same size as a small adult human. It weighs between 70 to 130 pounds and can be just over 5 feet tall.

Chimpanzees are covered with black hair but have a bare face, fingers, toes, palms, and feet.

## Gettin' Around

Chimpanzees spend time up in trees and on the ground. They can walk for short distances on their hind feet, but most of the time, they walk using their hands and feet.

New roads make it easier for poachers to get to chimps.

# ASIAN JUNGLES

The jungles of Asia are filled with unique species. There are strange, smelly plants, and creepy, crawly beasts. These jungles host some of the most beautiful animals on Earth as well. Unfortunately, some of these beautiful creatures are in big trouble.

## Big Cat

The tiger is the biggest cat on Earth. Its body can be more than seven feet long and over three feet tall at the shoulders. Male tigers are bigger than females. Males can weigh up to 500 pounds, while females sometimes weigh over 300 pounds.

# BENGAL TIGER

The Bengal tiger lives in the jungles and forests of India and a few nearby countries. In the wild, Bengal tigers live mainly on their own.

The fur of the Bengal tiger is striking. It's light orange or yellow with dark brown to black stripes. Its furry face, belly, ears, and legs are white. The coloring of its fur is good camouflage. It helps the tigers stay hidden while tracking prey. But the fur is in high demand from poachers. Poaching and habitat loss have made the Bengal tiger an endangered species.

## White Tiger

Some Bengal tigers have white fur with black stripes. These tigers are less common than the orange or yellow types.

# ASIAN ELEPHANT

The Asian elephant is smaller than its African cousin.  But it still weighs in at over 10,000 pounds.  It lives in many kinds of forests and grasslands in Asia.  It eats grasses and plants—up to 330 pounds each day!  Elephants are known for their trunks.  Eating is just one thing elephants use their trunks for.

Elephants are also admired for their tusks.  They are used for many purposes, including digging for water, fighting, and breaking branches from trees.  Asian elephants like to live in groups.  But that doesn't protect them from poachers, who kill them for their tusks.  The elephants are also endangered by deforestation, which is causing their homes to disappear.

An Asian elephant's skin can be more than an inch thick.

Elephants use their trunks for breathing, drinking, feeding, touching, dusting, communicating, washing, pinching, grasping, and fighting.

## Vulnerable Cousin

The African elephant is at risk for the same reasons as the Asian elephant. It is the largest living land animal. Males can be up to 13 feet tall and weigh up to 13,330 pounds.

## Jumbo

Asian elephant males can weigh up to 12,000 pounds and be up to 10 feet tall at the shoulder, while females weigh up to 9,200 pounds and can be more than 8 feet tall at the shoulder.

## Invisible Losses

If a large animal, such as an elephant, is endangered, researchers know about the problem. They are easy to count, and it's easy to see when their numbers decline. But some of the most worrisome losses are those animals we never even knew existed. The jungle is home to millions of undiscovered species—big and small. There is no way of knowing how many of these undiscovered creatures have been lost. But what if one of them might have given humans ideas that would improve our lives?

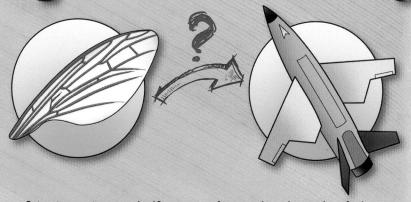

Scientists estimate only 40 percent of insects have been identified. What if the wings of a lost insect could have inspired a new spaceship design?

In recent years, scientists have discovered a pink dolphin, a bald parrot and a furry crab. What will they find next?

In the last 10 years, researchers have found over 1,200 species in the Amazon jungle alone. What if an undiscovered monkey could provide clues about human relationships?

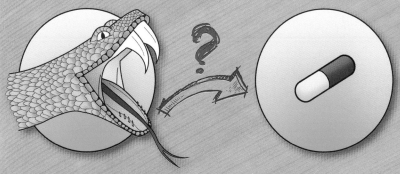

The venom of an undiscovered snake may hold clues for creating new types of medicine.

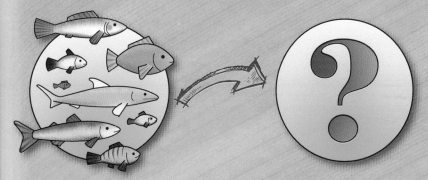

There are hundreds of fish still to be discovered in the rivers of the jungle. Researchers say there may be too many fish and too little time to find them all.

# GIANT PANDA

The giant panda is a type of bear. It lives in China. Pandas are known for their unique black-and-white fur. They live alone except during breeding season. The giant panda is threatened by habitat loss and a very low birthrate. Poachers want its fur. **Conservation** efforts have helped increase the number of pandas in the wild.

Although pandas are often shown in photographs up in trees, they actually spend most of their time on the ground.

Pandas have five fingers and a "thumb" on their paws. The thumb is a special bone that helps pandas hold bamboo while eating.

## The Panda's Diet

Although pandas are bears, they mainly eat bamboo, as much as 30 pounds each day. Pandas have round faces shaped by their powerful jaw muscles, which help them crush and grind the fibrous bamboo material.

## Malayan Sun Bear

The Malayan sun bear, also called a honey bear, is vulnerable to poaching and human development. This small bear lives primarily in tropical rainforests. It uses its long tongue to get honey from beehives. The sun bear does not see very well, but it uses its strong sense of smell to find food. It has a pale-orange-yellow marking on its chest that looks like a sunburst.

# LAR GIBBON

The lar gibbon is a type of ape. Its fur ranges from sandy to black. But its hands, feet, and fur around its face are white. The lar gibbon spends most of its time in trees. It eats fruit, leaves, insects, flowers, and sometimes bird eggs.

The lar gibbon is endangered by loss of habitat from human development. Humans also hunt the primate for food. Sadly, sometimes the parents are killed so the babies can be captured and kept as pets.

## Toothy

Both the male and the female lar gibbon have very large, sharp canine teeth. The teeth can be used for defense against predators and opponents. Other female gibbons and primates usually do not have such large, sharp teeth.

The lar gibbon lives mainly in the forests of Southeast Asia.

## Jungle Acrobats

Many people consider lar gibbons to be the fastest and most agile primates in the trees. They have long arms and are strong brachiators, meaning they move themselves through the forest by swinging from branch to branch with their arms. They may sometimes "fly" up to 40 or 50 feet between branches.

# PHILIPPINE EAGLE

The Philippine eagle lives mainly in the Philippines. This bird has brown and white feathers and a shaggy **crest** that looks like a lion's mane. It's a large, powerful bird with strong legs and large claws. It's fast and agile in flight. This eagle is seriously endangered by habitat loss and deforestation. Pollution and poaching are other big threats.

This bird is also known as the *monkey-eating eagle.*

## Big Eater

Despite being known as the *monkey-eating eagle*, this bird also eats other large animals such as flying foxes, large snakes, and other large birds. There have even been reports of Philippine eagles taking young pigs and small dogs!

The life expectancy for Philippine eagles in the wild is between 30 to 60 years.

# QUEEN ALEXANDRA BIRDWING BUTTERFLY

The Queen Alexandra birdwing butterfly is found mainly in Papua New Guinea. It is the largest butterfly in the world. Females can have a wingspan of up to 12 inches!

The butterfly is endangered from habitat loss. This is because of human development and a large volcanic eruption in 1951. Collectors seek the birdwing. They may pay thousands of dollars for one butterfly. But it's against the law to sell them.

## Territorial Males

Male birdwing butterflies are powerful fliers and highly **territorial**. They patrol their areas and chase off other male butterflies and even small birds.

Adult birdwing butterflies may live for three months or more.

Females, which are larger than males, are less colorful, too. They have mainly brown wings with white spots, while the male's wings are brown with large shimmery blue and green patches.

## Birdwing Babies

Female birdwing butterflies may lay up to 27 eggs during their lifetime. They lay their eggs on a specific type of plant called a *pipe vine*, which has a flower shaped like a pipe. The larvae eat parts of the pipe vine after hatching from their eggs.

Orangutans mainly eat fruit but also eat plant leaves, insects, honey, and bird eggs.

# ORANGUTAN

Orangutans have long brown-orange fur. They spend most of their time in trees. They use their long, strong arms to swing gently and confidently between branches. They use their feet like a second pair of hands.

Orangutans don't live in groups like other primates. After the first two or three years of life, they mainly live alone. But they can survive very well. They make tools and build cozy shelters.

Threats to orangutans include poaching, habitat destruction, and being captured and sold as illegal pets. But there are many people working to help orangutans survive in Borneo and Sumatra.

The bigger **dominant** males have large cheek pads and make long hooting calls to attract females and scare off other large males.

## High Intelligence

When tested by scientists, orangutans have shown the ability to solve difficult problems. They can even play computer games.

# SOUTH AMERICAN JUNGLES

South American jungles are home to some of the most interesting species on the planet. But habitat loss and other threats endanger many of these species. Despite their low numbers, these unique creatures are unforgettable.

## MANED THREE-TOED SLOTH

The maned three-toed sloth lives in trees in the coastal rainforests of Brazil. It gets its name from the long black hair covering its neck and shoulders. Sloths are known for their very slow movements. They may spend up to 80 percent of their time sleeping! Sloths hang from tree branches with their long claws and rarely come down. When they do, they cannot stand or walk. They drag themselves along the ground.

The sloth is at risk from hunting. It is also losing its habitat to lumber, farming, and cattle operations.

Maned sloths have pale-brown to gray fur with shorter black and white underfur and a small head with a mask of black hair.

## Friends in Their Fur

Many living things make their home in a sloth's coarse outer fur. Mites, ticks, beetles, moths, and algae can all be found there.

# GOLDEN-LION TAMARIN

The golden-lion tamarin is a small monkey that lives in the rainforests of Brazil. It gets its name from its brightly colored fur and the long fur around its face.

Adult tamarins have tails that are longer than their bodies. But they cannot use their tails to grab things as other monkeys can. They run and jump along branches as they move through the trees. They move more like squirrels than other monkeys that swing between branches.

Logging, poaching, and mining are all endangering the tamarin.

## Primate with Claws

Like other monkeys from North and South America, golden-lion tamarins have claw-like fingernails. These help them climb and hold onto trees and branches as they move around in the jungle.

The golden-lion tamarin is also known as the *golden marmoset*.

Small groups of 8 to 10 tamarins live together. They are **omnivores**, but they mainly eat fruits, flowers, and nectar.

The large spotted jaguar looks very much like a leopard but is bigger and stronger. The adult lives alone except when breeding.

Jaguars are at the top of the food chain. Jaguars help maintain balance in the jungle. Their hunts prevent other animals from taking over. Because jungles are being threatened, the jaguars are in danger, too. Habitat loss is killing off the jaguar, and so are farmers and ranchers who kill jaguars to protect their livestock.

Jaguars use a stalk-and-ambush hunting style.

## Swimming Cat?

If you have a pet cat, you probably know most cats do not like to swim or even get wet. Most cats in the wild are the same way. However, jaguars appear to like the water and, like tigers, are good swimmers.

Jaguars live in the dense jungles and forest areas of Central and South America. They have mainly been extirpated from North America.

Jaguars are known for their powerful jaws. They can even bite through turtle shells!

# HYACINTH MACAW

The hyacinth macaw is a parrot that lives in the jungles of South America. The macaw's feathers are blue. It has a small ring of yellow skin around its eyes and next to its beak. Its black beak is strong and curved. It can even crack coconuts and large nuts.

Macaws prefer to live in the open parts of the jungle where it is easier to fly. These beautiful birds are mainly endangered by the loss of their habitats and the illegal pet trade.

## Big Bird

Adult hyacinth macaws can reach a length of just over three feet from the tip of the head to the tip of the tail. That makes them the largest macaws and the largest flying parrots in the world.

# NORTH AMERICAN JUNGLES

The Olympic Rainforest in Washington State is the only jungle in North America. One species there has become the symbol for all endangered species in the area.

## MARBLED MURRELET

The marbled murrelet lives in the forests and seas of Washington State. It nests in the large trees of old-growth forests. It feeds in the surrounding ocean. This small bird has a slender black bill. Its feathers change colors from season to season. Experts think it is endangered because logging is destroying its habitat.

In summer, the murrelet has brown speckled feathers.

Changing ocean climate conditions are also now considered to be a cause for the murrelet's endangered status.

Both the male and female murrelet share responsibility for warming and protecting their eggs until they hatch.

# WAYS TO HELP

It's important to everyone—people and animals alike—that we do what we can to protect endangered species. We're making progress already. Of the species that were listed as endangered in the 1970s, over 60 percent are stable today. But most researchers think the worst losses are still to come. And the most important work is still ahead of us.

The National Wildlife Federation is just one of many organizations that work to protect animals.

## Help Out

Talk with your family about organizations that work to protect the environment and help threatened and endangered animal populations recover. Contact the organizations to see how you can help.

# So what can YOU do?

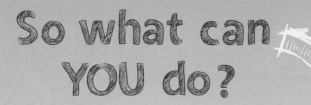

## Protect the Environment

Always remember the three Rs— **reduce, reuse, and recycle**. Practicing the three Rs goes a long way in helping the environment and many animal species.

## Protect Habitats

You can plant native flowers for bees and nectar-eating birds. Avoid polluting forests and nearby waterways.

# Who's Making a Difference?

Many people around the world are working to protect endangered species and their environments. Some were early heroes of the movement. Others are still leading the way today. Learn who they are—and maybe you will want to join them, too!

## World Wildlife Fund for Nature

**www.wwf.org**

The World Wildlife Fund (WWF) is an international non-governmental organization that works to conserve, study, and restore the environment. It has over 5 million supporters working in more than 100 countries around the world. It focuses on the conservation of three biomes: forests, freshwater **ecosystems**, and oceans and coastal areas.

## Good Friend to Gorillas

Dian Fossey studied gorillas for more than 18 years and was a strong advocate for protection of gorillas and other animals. She was killed in 1985 at the age of 53. Her murder has never been solved, although many people believe she was killed by gorilla poachers.

### Chimpanzee Champion

Jane Goodall is a well-known scientist who probably knows more about chimpanzees than any other person does. She has been studying chimps, mainly in Africa, for many years. She has written several books about her experiences and observations.

### Authority on Orangutans

Birute Galdikas was born in Germany and educated in North America. She has studied orangutans for more than 30 years and is considered to be a leading authority on them. Prior to her field studies, scientists knew very little about them. Much of what people know about orangutans comes from her fieldwork, with the support of the National Geographic Society.

# Making a Difference

# GLOSSARY

**abandoned**—to withdraw protection, support, or help from

**agile**—quick and well-coordinated

**agriculture**—the science or occupation of farming

**camouflage**—protective fur or skin coloring that lets an animal blend with its surroundings

**carnivores**—animals that eat only meat

**conservation**—the protection of plant and animal species and the environment

**crest**—a plume of feathers along the top of the head

**deforestation**—the clearing away of forests and trees

**dominant**—commanding or having great influence over others

**ecosystems**—all the plants, animals, and other elements of a particular area

**endangered**—threatened and at risk of extinction

**erosion**—the gradual destruction of something by natural forces such as water, wind, or ice

**exotic**—foreign to a particular area

**extinct**—no longer living or in existence

**extirpated**—extinct within a local area, but existing elsewhere

**fertile**—able to produce life

**fossils**—the remains, impressions, or traces of living things from long ago

**fungi**—a group of organisms that include mushrooms, molds, and yeasts

**habitat**—a natural living environment

**native**—naturally belonging to an area

**omnivores**—animals that eat both meat and plants

**organisms**—living people, plants, or animals

**poached**—to have illegally killed or stolen an animal, usually for some financial gain

**population**—a group of one or more species of organisms living in a particular area or habitat

**primate**—an animal, including apes and humans, with flexible hands and feet, opposable thumbs, good eyesight, and a highly developed brain

**renewable**—able to be restored

**species**—a specific animal group with common characteristics

**sustained**—ongoing continuously

**taxonomy**—orderly classification of plants and animals according to their presumed natural relationships

**territorial**—highly protective of the area in which one lives and apt to chase away intruders

**thrive**—to grow vigorously

# INDEX

# BIBLIOGRAPHY

Bortolotti, Dan. *Panda Rescue: Changing the Future for Endangered Wildlife.* Firefly Books, 2003.

Step into the bamboo forest, home of the beloved panda. This book opens your eyes to the dangers faced by the panda and includes ways you can help, too.

Cohn, Jessica. *Hand to Paw: Protecting Animals.* Teacher Created Materials, 2013.

There are so many ways that people can help keep animals safe from danger. Learn about various animals and what we can do to help them. Find out about career paths that allow people to help animals for a living.

Holsey, Kellie. *The Secret Sloth.* Winter Goose Publishing, 2011.

Hang out and get to know the amazing sloth. The hand-drawn sketches bring to life this intriguing animal. A portion of the proceeds from this book will go to support the organization Kids Saving the Rainforest.

Radley, Gail. *Vanishing from Forests and Jungles.* Carolrhoda Books, 2001.

Jungle animals are some of the most exquisite and diverse animals on the planet. But some of them are in danger of extinction. This book includes information and a map describing the lives and whereabouts of 10 endangered jungle animals. It also includes a poem for each animal.

# MORE TO EXPLORE

## Amazon Rainforest

*http://www.sheppardsoftware.com/content/animals/kidscorner/endangered_animals/endangeredanimals_1.htm*

Find out more about some of the Amazon's endangered animals such as the jaguar, golden-lion tamarin, and poison-dart frog. You will also learn about the problems facing them and how you can help.

## Kids Saving the Rainforest

*http://www.kidssavingtherainforest.org/main.html*

Join Janine and her friends as they work to save the rainforest. You can "adopt" trees and animals and donate toward the treatment of sick or injured rainforest animals.

## Kids for Forests

*http://archive.greenpeace.org/kidsforforests/about.html*

Stand up for Earth's remaining ancient forests and the animals that call them home. Help bring attention to the shrinking forest through creative projects and writing letters.

## Endangered Animals Quiz

*http://animals.nationalgeographic.com/animals/endangered-animals-quiz*

Do you know how many big cats have gone extinct in your lifetime? Test your knowledge of endangered animals with this quiz. You may be surprised what you find out.

# ABOUT THE AUTHOR

William B. Rice grew up in Pomona, California, and graduated from Idaho State University with a degree in geology. He works at a California state agency that strives to protect the quality of surface and groundwater resources. Protecting and preserving the environment is important to him. William is married with two children and lives in Southern California.